I'm still healing, okay?

Juice

BookLeaf Publishing
India | USA | UK

Presentation by *BookLeaf Publishing*

Web: www.bookleafpub.com

E-mail: info@bookleafpub.com

ISBN: 9789363301337

First edition 2024

For my niece ZuZu,

Because of you, the world is more beautiful.

ACKNOWLEDGEMENT

First I want to give honor and thanks to my God. She is gracious and giving. Everything that I have ever needed, You have shown me I already had within myself. You have never left me. Even in my darkest moments, You revealed the light within me to guide my way.

To my mom, thank you for teaching me to always speak my mind— though I'm sure you didn't expect it to sometimes be against you, lol.

Thank you, Mackkkkkkk— Ms. Mackenzie Malkemes! The best English teacher I've ever had! Thank you for introducing me to spoken word and for being the first person to care about me using the power of my voice. I freaking love you, girl! You changed my life; you saved my life. I'm forever grateful!

To Kane Smego and CJ Suitt, two of the most incredible poets I've ever met. My brothers and my mentors! Thank you for all the hours spent editing my poems and coaching me. I can only hope to one day be as great as y'all!

To every friend, family member, or stranger who's given me feedback on anything I've written or performed, thank you.

To BookLeaf Publishing, thank you for this amazing opportunity. It has meant so much to me!

PREFACE

Y'all, I am so glad to finally be published! I've been writing since before I could even spell properly, and one of my biggest goals has always been to write a book— even if no one ever reads it. I spent most of my life with my head lost in the pages of a book, hoping that someday, someone would find my words just as powerful as the ones I treasured.

Growing up, I was really shy— the kind of shy where I barely said much at all. Writing became my only refuge. When I was first introduced to spoken word, I dove headfirst into that world. Constant workshops, open mics, and slam competitions became my life. But once I aged out of youth activities, I struggled to transition into being an adult performer. Suddenly, the scoring felt way more serious, and the love for your art came with limits if someone saw you as competition. I started putting so much pressure on myself that I lost sight of what mattered most to me: being my most authentic self with my art and using it to heal myself.

It pushed me away from writing for a long time when I should have just taken a break from competing. I don't regret it, though. What I do regret is believing my words weren't worthy of being told— or that they needed to be "pretty" to be appreciated.

To be completely honest, writing this was hard. It had been so long since I had written, and I've grown so much that I didn't even recognize my own voice. I kept scrapping poems, trying to get back to my old self and recapture that rhythm of magic that I used to swim through. But that was my first mistake— I am not her anymore, and I never will be. And who's to say that this version of me is not good enough? Rubbish!

I wrote this while dealing with grief, depression, emotional abuse, and so much more. And nobody, not even myself, is going to tell me that this woman I am right now is not enough!

Writing this has unlocked that flowing river in my chest again— that deep need to be heard and to tell a story. I am hoping to be published more in the future. Right now, I am working on a zombie apocalypse story. And yes, y'all, there will be black characters! LOL!

This is for everyone who looks like me, for everyone who has ever woken up and wanted to go back to sleep forever. For the girls who were left alone with the wrong family members. For the people who think they can't leave or prosper on their own. I see you. I hear you. I am you! And I love you.

Thank you!

- Juice

Sun Rays

Before she met him, she used to go everywhere!
And everywhere she went, she had to look like
she had somewhere important to be, and she just
happened to stumble in.
Post office? Makeup, of course!
Grocery store? A fresh re-twist!
Her scalp would be so greased you could see
your reflection in herself.
She used to laugh loudly.
So loud, she couldn't even be embarrassed by
the pig snort that would shove its way out.
That kind of loud that you didn't even have to
know what was funny but you'd laugh too!
Loud enough for her to make you feel like you
were free.

And you could tell she was, too, because her
dimples would rise on both sides of her face,
Her smile resembling an angel spreading its
wings and flying for the first time.
Because she was free,
Because nothing could tie her down,
She wore clothes to only dress her body.
She didn't allow her attire to hold her body
down.
Thighs jiggled when she walked,
Titties danced out of her shirts.
She'd trained her ears to listen to what felt good
on her skin and ignored the false messages her
mind would sometimes send to her eyes.
Her reflection was a true passenger princess,
never setting foot in the driver's seat of what she
thought was beautiful.
And boy, was she beautiful.
Not only the outside, but it was the inside that
shined,
The inside that shone such a bright light, it
made everyone else yearn to be around her.
She was used to that.
Used to everyone basking in her sunlight,
Browning themselves and shading when they'd
reached their desires.
He yearned for her light as well.
At first, he thought he could handle it.

He’d stand in her rays, skin sizzling like the heat
she used to feel from grandmama’s hot comb.
Skin blistered, welts completely covering his
face, so that his reflection would never allow
him to forget that in her light, he could not stand.
How could he truly be a man if she shined
brighter than him?
He didn’t know how,
Refused to learn
He couldn’t.
He no longer yearned for her brightness.
He yearned to control it,
Dim it to his will.
Soon, her going out seemed like she was never
happy being inside with him.
Her dressing up seemed like her wanting to
out-style him.
Her laugh, her loud, beautiful laugh, became a
weapon that he believed was only brought out to
silence him
Soon it seemed like her body was only present to
piss him off.
Her eyes believed those false messages her mind
sent.
That passenger princess started creeping into the
driver's seat,
Steering herself straight into his midnight soul.
He couldn’t help that he never lit up on his own.
He didn’t know how,

So she dimmed herself down,
Quieted her loud laugh,
Burdened herself with the heaviness.
She figured that even the sun had to set sometimes,
Giving the moon it's time to be the only one dreamed for.
It couldn’t exist in the sun's rays anyway.
It didn’t know how.
It refused to learn.
It just couldn’t.

Ira

Today is one of those days where anger isn't
enough.
Sooner or later, being mad about the same shit
feels repetitive.
Shouting does nothing when no one ever bothers
to listen.
It cages me in,
A room with no doors,
Walls covered floor to ceiling with monitors,
A never-ending show of all the times someone
has had me fucked up.
It gets heavy,
This anger,
Belly fat with insults I want to hurl at everyone
who wrongs me.
Fingers chubby with all the rage I won't let fly
into someone's face.
I've gotten used to the boiling,
A pot close to overflowing,
Liquid that evaporates just enough that only
steam sizzles over the edge.
My toxic trait is that I love the burn.
I cling to the heated bubbles,
Cumming to the steady drum of hatred in my
veins.

The pain feels like the only thing I can control,
The only thing that fills me up.
It has to be enough.
Today, I'm angry.
And it's the only thing that I have.

???

Why is it that dudes still don't know how to eat
pussy?
I mean, you can spend 48 hours with a game
controller in your hand
Yet still be rubbing my clit like it's a $2
scratch-off ticket.
It deeply disturbs me.
I mean, you like head, right?
And expect me to abide by all your rules?
"Stick your ass out, no teeth, now no hands!
Oh, and don't forget about the balls."
Yet when it's your turn,
You're all lost, like my vagina is on the other
side of Narnia.
And why do you say if it's got hair on it, you
ain't eating it?
But your pubes are longer than Michael
Jackson's jerry curl.
Why do you stroke for 2 minutes and
then have the nerve to ask:
"Did you cum, baby?"
No, you selfish mothafucka!
Why, when I'm on my period, do I gotta suck
your dick?

My vagina bleeding, my stomach’s in knots, and my head hurts too!
Why do you want a threesome with me, you, and Keshia?
But when I ask can Trey join, it’s a problem?
Why do you make one girl cum and think that weak-ass stroke game is some pressure?
Why don't you know a lot of women need more than penetration to orgasm?
Why do you wanna go raw, but when I text you I’m late, it ain’t yours?
Why do you gotta lie to get the draws?
Why you want one-night stands
But a woman that’s open with her sexuality is either
Unattractive to you, a hoe, or both?
Why can't you be honest about what you want?
Why do you want no strings attached
But keep fucking women who want real love?
Why do you lie about who you are to get with me?
Show me your true colors,
Then blame me for having poor choices in men?
Why are you trash?
Why are you trash?
Why are you trash?
Why are you ready to kill the boy who broke your daughter’s heart
When he’s just being a man

Like you?
Why do you still think it’s a man's world
When pussy is the heaven you come from?
Why you fuck over good women when you’re young,
Call it “learning,”
Then mature,
Ready for something serious?
Those good women, now “hoes,” from your “learning,”
And you can’t see why there’s no more “real women” left?
Why do you still think this poem is just about eating pussy?
Why can't you see that you’re toxic?
Why can't you see that I see that you’re toxic?
Why are you mad that I know you’re toxic?
Again, I ask,
Why do you still think it’s a man's world?
Like we need you
Like we’d be clueless without you?
Why you don’t know that from the day we’re born,
We’re taught how to live without you,
Raise your kids without you,
Shit, even cum without you?
Still think this poem isn’t talking about you?
Why you got certain requirements but me having standards means:

I wouldn't know a "good man" when I see one
Why do I gotta have a Coke bottle shape, be close to a virgin, have a car, own a place, and no kids
When all you can offer is consistent dick, a 20% chance of an orgasm, a UTI, and constant headaches?
Why, with all your flaws,
Why do we still respect you?
Love you?
And be here for you in ways you can't do the same for us?
We deal with it,
Take it for what it is,
Even though this isn't what it should be.
With all of that, I ask,
Why is it that dudes still don't know how to eat pussy?

Dear Gloria

Dear Gloria,

I thought about your last letter,
I can't lie, it brought tears to my eyes.
To Know you're carrying my son is a
blessing I never thought I deserved.
I always dreamed of a Jr., little league,
And a small ass pair of Timbs for my
boy.

To be in here, while you out there,
Is a pain I couldn't even begin to
describe.
I Know I promised better days,
Yet all I brought to you was pain,
And I regret that.
For you to hear his heartbeat,
For me to read about his heartbeat,
I regret that.
To have to see my Kids through a glass
I regret that.

I never wanted you to be my mother.
Young, single, pregnant, and broKe,
That Killed me.

Hearing you say I'm selfish,
That Killed me.
I'm the one in the cage, and you're
sweating me?
LiKe where I'm sitting is the best seat in
this situation?
LiKe what do you Know about being a
man?

What do you know about that kind of
pressure?
You'll never understand.
I had my first daughter at 16,
Had to get that money by any means.
No father, my mother had 3 kids,
And looked at me to take over.
The streets put clothes on my back
when my parents couldn't.
I made a promise my kids would never
see this life.
It ain't easy being a man out here.
Come home, and you gotta be a man in
the house too.
Ya girl demanding, and start tripping.
Bills demanding, and start flipping,
Until you can't hear your thoughts.
Don't get me wrong, I'm here because of
me,
But I'm also in here for trying to provide
for my family.
Like, what do you know about being a
man?
Being a black man?
America's most hated,

Most duplicated,
And never appreciated.
We are dying out here.
They can paint the city red in our blood,
It's our bodies lying in the street,
And that ain't just from us Killing each other.
That's from being hunted too.
You Know about being a black man?
A target?
Fatherless?
A felon?
You Know that Kind of pain?
When it's destined for you
From the womb.
I tried to fight it,
Tried school,
Tried to work,
Tried the right way.
But how you put that you've been to more funerals than graduations on a job application?
How do you explain Keeping the lights on and feeding your Kids with drug money?

How do you walk away when checking the "I've been to jail" box closes all your doors?
But I'm selfish?
You ain't dealing with the things I'm dealing with, and that's real shit.

P.S. Give my babies a kiss for me.

Dear Hakeem

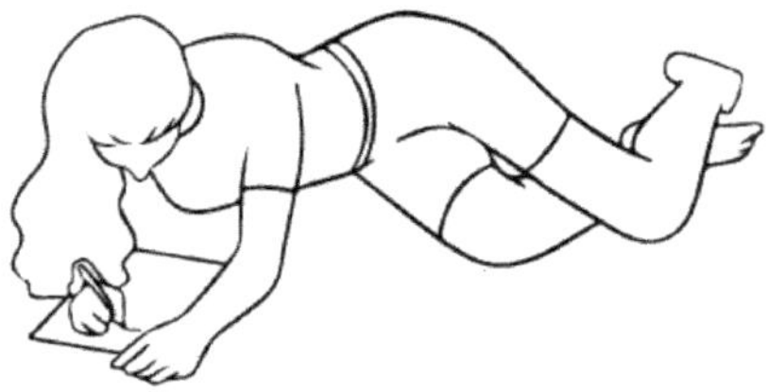

Dear Hakeem,

I read your letter,
And for you to spend so much time in a box alone,
You're still as selfish as before you left.
You think you're the only one in these streets?
Like your blood is the only one being shed?
Who do you think cleans that up?
We do.
Black women.
We clean up your blood,
Raise your fatherless children,
And become men in households where we bet not dare complain.

I never wanted to be your mother.

Young, single, pregnant, and broke.

You know what it's like to be a woman?

To be a woman and to be black?

To be abused and disrespected by men who don't look like you,

And to share that same disrespect with men who do?

You telling me you got it hard like I don't know?

Like I'm not the one you take it out on?

You're selfish.

You call it providing for us,

That's what got you in here.

But what about now?

Who's taking care of your kids?

Not you.

Who's helping me keep a roof over our heads?

Not you.

You were fatherless, now you're leaving your kids to feel that same pain.

You think you're the only one in prison?

I'm pregnant by a man I may never see again
without bars or glass in front of his face.
I live in fear of my children, or even me, not living
to see tomorrow.
I work hard to support my community only to be
called names by men made to protect me.
Trust me, we all have it hard out here.
Not just you.
Not just men.
The difference is women have been holding y'all up
for years,
And some of us have even died trying to protect
each other.
Because when it's our time,
You can't even show up.
Too busy stuck in a cell that's far worse than
prison–
The black man's pity party on being the worst off.
That was your cell way before you ended up in jail.

P.S. I'm still praying for you.

To my aunt

A letter to my aunt who knew her son was molesting me and didn't stop it:

Do you remember those ninja turtle bed sheets
you bought Man for his bunk bed?
I do.
I still remember the taste of his pillow,
as his game controller hands rolled over my 7
year old body.
Cotton melted like heated plastic on my tongue
It's sunny outside.
I can hear you in the living room, yelling at your
home girl on the phone.
Man is shoving his tongue down my throat.
I can hear you in the living room, yelling at your
home girl on the phone.
Man has his hand down my pants.
I can hear you in the living room, yelling at your
home girl on the phone.

Your daughter walks in on us.
I can hear her in the hallway, yelling to you,
eyes 2 dancing fire dragons

It took me years to take my body back from him.
It's taken me my whole life to not take others.
Did you know, around 30% of sexually abused
victims turn into abusers?
How easy it is to give pain when trying to get rid
of it.

Do you remember the marble tiles you bought
for you and your husband's new kitchen?
Flesh ripped open as decoration.
This was the first time you'd purchased a resting
place for your beaten body.
Blood probably tastes a lot like cotton.
How could he tear down a home that was never
his?
It's dark outside.
You can hear his fist echoing in the kitchen,
pounding your house of a body.
You've been threatening to leave him.
You can hear his fist echoing in the kitchen,
pounding your house of a body.
You're pregnant again.
You can hear his fist echoing in the kitchen,
pounding your house of a body.
Your daughter walks in on y'all.

You can hear her in the hallway, yelling to you,
eyes 2 cubs witnessing bullets ripping through
their mother's flesh.

It took you years to get away from this man, too
bad he stuck his demon in your womb.
I've been trying to get away from him too.
Do you see your husband in your son?
Do you see yourself in me?
Do you remember those ninja turtle bed sheets?
Do they remind you of that old marble floor?
Blood probably tastes a lot like cotton.
Smells familiar, feels familiar.

Did you know, around 30% of sexually abused
victims turn into abusers?
How easy it is to give pain when trying to get rid
of it.
How easy it is to look away when no one
bothered to look at you

The repetitive trauma that we cycle through our
villages can be stopped

So I pray to my future daughter who will know
of blood
but shall never taste it.

War

I can't feel my soul anymore.
Can't feel my body.
Can't figure out when I will wake up from this recurring nightmare.
Another one of us,
Dead.
Another one of us ain't come home last night
Another one of our mothers won't be sleeping for a long time.
And I,
Am forgetting how to feel.
Hands shaking,
10 and 2 on the steering wheel.
The fear
That a broken tail light will turn into a 2 a.m. phone call to my mother:
"I'm sorry, Ms. Hemingway,
But this is daughter #2 for you to bury"
I can never watch the news
Can't stomach the 1,000+ black dead bodies they've been feeding us this year.
Don't wanna hear anymore: hands up, don't shoot.
They've been killing us with our backs turned anyway.

Tired of having to explain #BlackLivesMatter to
these white folks who play victim every chance
they get.
Constantly complaining about how hard their
lives are.
You know:
Getting pulled over by the police and surviving
long enough to see the inside of the courtroom.
How all lives matter, yet white murders are
being solved.
20 plus years later,
We're still wondering what really happened to
Biggie and Tupac.
How blacks are ghetto and unprofessional
Yet every time we make something clever here
comes
Becky the black trend stealer with her handy
dandy notebook
Ready to steal some shit with no clue about the
culture behind it.
You say "Bye Felicia,"
Yet you still think *Friday* is just a day of the
week.
I can't remember feeling anything but pain,
Anger,
Resentment.
Trying to see it's not all of them,
But it's really most of them.
Tired of being Martin

and feeling more like Malcolm.
Feels like war.
Feels like the only way to be heard is to take one of theirs.
Got me feeling like Malcolm at the front door,
Shotgun in hand,
The Black Panthers in '68,
Ferguson after Michael Brown,
Baltimore after Freddie,
The country after George Floyd!
The world after Breonna Taylor!
Ain't no more #BlackLivesMatter, bitch.
It's
#Killanotheroneofusandwatchwhathappenstoyou
rbitch ass!
I can't remember feeling anything but pain.
My melanin doesn't allow me to be celebrated.
Can't swim in my own neighborhood without my bikini posing a threat.
Can't make the mistake of not putting on my turning signal without being murdered.
Can't walk home with a bag of Skittles and some tea.
Can't be black.
Can't be black.
Can't be black.
Can't be black.
They've forced me to believe that the only thing I can do is hurt and attack.

That’s fine
That just means the war,
Has now begun.

To my sister

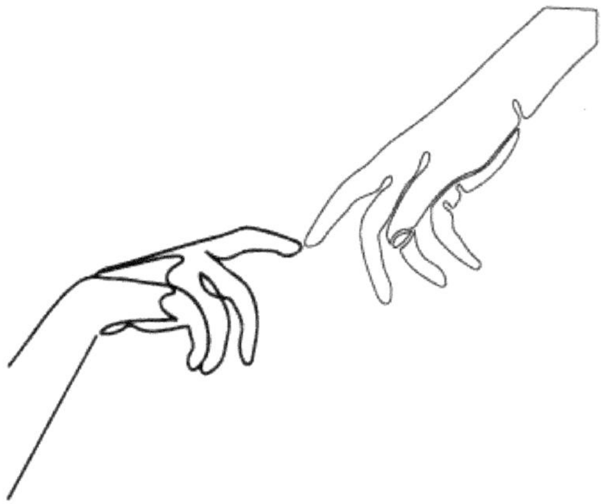

To my little sister who thinks I hate her,
When somebody has been molesting you; your whole life, do you call it love?
When anxiety nestles in your stomach from the hands you didn't want touching you, do you call it excitement?
When you find yourself sneaking around with the person who tricked you into thinking that secrets are better left hidden in the sheets of a family member's bed, do you call it a romantic love affair?
I'm sorry, I never learned how to show emotions with actions.

Never quite noticed the warning signs before falling off of a cliff, I've always latched on to things that were no good for me anyway.
Love and leave, leave and love, stay and hurt.
I can still feel my older cousin touching my 7 year old body,
then my teenage body,
then my adult body.
Still smell his scent like it was yesterday. The smell of burnt childhood memories and hushed up confessions. Still feel his eyes, searching for any innocence I may have left.
Living in a house of 3 children, but only sharing a father with 1. I felt over protective of you! Caught between being the middle child, yet still being the oldest. Forgive me, for not having time to exchange "I love you's" between picking up ancient grenades in your battlefield of a childhood and trying to make sure you still grow up to be half as woman as me.
How lucky, to still call yourself a child, to be pure, to have your innocence, to not be affected by our family's secrets. My skeletons were never in my closet, they've always been in my blood line. While you balleted through your reality fairytales, I had to tell myself that touching a child wasn't the right way to show affection. You don't know how it feels to think you're part monster and part human.

Baby sister, I could never know how to love. Don't know what it feels like when somebody's trying to love me. Love and leave, leave and love, stay and abandon. Relationships have never come easy to me, love has never given me a reason to trust it. I've watched bastards come into my life with cheap father costumes! I've learned your family, isn't your family unless one of them is fucking you. Love is breaking someone down and building them up how you want them to be. Killing everything they believe in, until all they have is you. I'm 30 years old, and my rearview mirror is filled with half burned images of a childhood I never wanted to face, of a family blaming me for being molested, instead of telling me it's not okay to molest. How do you know when something's wrong, when you were never told it's not right? Right and wrong, wrong and right. They've always looked the same to me. Growing up with this disease of the mind, I felt like I needed to protect you from me. Baby sister, if love is breaking someone down and building them up how you want them to be. Then hate, hate shall be beautiful

High functioning depression

......

I can't even write anymore.
I've been faking the funk, hiding how I feel for so long that I do know what's real anymore.
Overthinking constantly.
Stuck in a consistent loop.
Feeling empty—
But somehow feeling full at the same time.
Wanting to scream—
But craving the too
Wanting to be heard and understood—
Yet terrified of the vulnerability that comes with sharing.
Wanting real happiness—
But convincedI don't deserve it.

Wanting it to end—
But still hoping to try again tomorrow.
A lot of pain.
A lot of happy memories, too.
And that's the part that fucks me up.
Is it real?
Or is it just real in my head?

To the girl that I was before abuse

At first, it'll feel real—
Genuine.
Sincere.
You won't see the red flags you should,
Because you'll want love.
Real love.
The kind you've been waiting for way longer
than you've even known what love truly is.
At first, it'll seem worth it—all the pain it
brings,
Worth the shame and the self-doubt.
At first, you'll think it's you,
That it's your fault, and that you deserve it all.
It'll seem too hard to let go,
Easier to stay, because you think you're used to
it.
Easier to deal with, because you've convinced
yourself you're not worth the struggle of
leaving.
It'll seem impossible to overcome,
Like you'll always be stuck,
Always feel low,
Always be lost,
Always be broken.

But you won’t.
One day, you’ll feel the brightness of the sun again,
Without the heaviness of chains holding you back.
One day, you’ll see your reflection,
And depression won’t cling to your shoulders.
One day, you’ll find the strength to leave, and it won’t be hard, it’ll be the easiest decision you’ve ever made.
One day, you’ll realize that someone else’s bad treatment of you is not a reflection of you.
Or your worth.
One day, you won’t be shamed.
Won’t be a victim.
Won’t blame you.
One day, you make yourself small so they can feel big.
One day, their insecurities won't be your battles anymore.
One day, you’ll choose you.

Changes

"I'm tired of being broke, and worse, I'm black.
My stomach aches, so I'm looking for a purse to snatch.
Cops give a damn about a Negro.
Pull the trigga, kill a nigga, he's a hero."

The sun doesn't shine no more, just black.
I've been looking for reasons to live, reasons to breathe,
Reasons not to carve my skin away with knives dripping with droplets of nothingness.

But it’s gotten hard, y'all.
Owning a brown body in this world means, even if you're not guilty, they’ll always prove you're not innocent.
There's something wrong when you find comfort in knowing your black skin matches the night, but feel fear in red and blue flashlights,
Spinning bright like lanterns dancing on dragging tree limbs &
reflecting off cuffed ankles.
The irony: when murdered black boys and rape victims share the same follow-up questions.
Us black folk, we’ve come a long way, y'all.
But the pigment of our skin becomes a ticking time bomb the moment we are born.
The darker we get, the more suspicious we become—
Needing escorts in the streets we call home,
Murdered in our backyards and trialed like aliens.
G-g-g-gunshots in rap songs become soundtracks to our funerals.
Rest-in-peace T-shirts waving like our American flag, stained with black blood.
You can find us on the corner, barely remembering Trayvon,
Michael's dead body printed across our hoodies like a fashionable crucifix,
while listening to a mixtape for Eric.

They say black folk stay trying to make everything a race issue, y'all.
Tell us no justice, poverty, and murder ain't got nothing to do with being black.
I'm so sick of being criticized for old habits we learned from others.
Done raped our babies, killed our young,
Tattooed "nigga" on the back of our throats so we'd never forget it.
Stripped us of our minds & said it was the "Christian thing."
They think because they've changed, the damage ain't already done.
Or is, "change" just the new word for covering shit up?
Prejudice no longer dances on pink lips due to curfew,
But it hangs on loaded guns when the sun no longer shines.
Syringes filled with ancestor hatred, so deep in their veins, they don't even realize they're racist
And it's sad.
Being in the land of the free but never free.
Cultures & roots being worn as trends.
Told when to be black & when not to be.
Told not to fight for justice, since it's just us committing the crimes.
They fear following our shadows, afraid of being swept by the darkness.

& I am the problem?
We are the problem?
You fear for your life momentarily,
while I fear for my life every day
Why was Skittles the last thing Hansel saw
while trying to find his way home?
I guess they don't print these stories.

I am a black woman, no longer afraid of what it means to be black.
Don't worry; you won't ever catch me "slipping."
I'm ready to fight, born to fight.
Momma said it won't be easy.
Don't do it because it's black; do it because love should break the bones of the hatred.

"I see no changes.
Wake up in the morning, & I ask myself: is life worth living? Should I blast myself?
I'm tired of being broke, and, even worse, I'm black.
My stomach hurts, so I'm looking for a purse to snatch.
Cops don't give a damn about a Negro.
Pull the trigga, kill a nigga, he's a hero "

For ZuZu

If there is ever a day or a moment you doubt
The brilliance you bring to this world,
Know that, there were civilizations that could
not see until your light shined on them.

Biological Dad

My dad passed away back in 2022.
We had a strained relationship—
And when I say strained, I mean
Carrying a big screen TV up 3 flights of stairs strained.
Strained like I had his name in my phone saved as "biological dad,"
Which was odd, because I didn't have any other dads.
But maybe I just needed it to remind myself of who he was,
Who he should have been.
My dad.
Instead of someone I used to avoid.
Someone who accused me of things I never did.
Someone who favored my sibling over me.
Someone who neglected me.
I cried so hard when I got the news.
Not because I lost my dad,
Because I lost ever having the opportunity of experiencing him *being* my dad.
I mourn the chance to feel
Unconditional love from him.
Understanding.
I mourn the chance for him to truly see me,

As Juice.
Or Jazz.
Not just Jasmine, but also Jasmine.
I mourn the chance to know him
As "dad," comfortable and open.
Not "Dad," hidden and guarded.
As Otis, and not BooBoo, which is what he hated.
Fresh regrets weigh on my heart,
With their guilty weight every time I think of him.
Yes, so many times I was wronged.
So many times he could, should have, stepped up.
Said something.
Done something.

When did the line push me
from being his child to an adult?
When did my choices in our strained
relationship turn into an obligation "to be grown"
and make a sound decision?
The overflow of scenarios that death brings
are endless rabbit holes for us to drown in.
It's possible my dad could have lived,
and we would have never been anything more.
But I mourn that too.
I mourn the possibility of nothingness.

I mourn knowing my dad
isn’t a phone call away anymore.

I just mourn.

Listening to God

When God shows you signs,
You close your eyes on purpose.
Crafting heartbreaks,
Your own design of hurt.

I Rebuke.

For Sonya Massey,
Who died in her nightgown
In the middle of her kitchen,
You are loved.
You are mourned.
You are not what's happened to you.
You are beautiful.
You are strong.
And you are not the last moments plastered on the internet.
I rebuke the demon who took you that night.
I rebuke the racism that entered your home and violated you.
I rebuke the man who treated you as trash because he could not handle your heavenly presence.
I rebuke the trauma placed on your son.
I rebuke whatever forces conspire to let your killer stand free.
I rebuke ever letting your name die.
Ms. Sonya,
You look like my mom,
My auntie,
My grandma,
My cousin,

My sister,
My friend.
Like me.
You look like so many people in my life,
And what kills me is knowing I'll see many
more familiar faces before this ends.
And I rebuke that, too.

Suicidal Thoughts

High functioning death.
Thoughts: wanting to die,
But not becoming a burden.

I am.

I am strong enough to leave.
I am strong enough to stand alone.
I am strong enough to choose me over him.
I am strong enough to say enough is enough
I am strong enough to love who I am,
No matter what he tells me.

Colors

They show their true colors.
Believe them when they do..
Don't paint them differently.

For Ahmaud Arbery

I've noticed how small I try to make myself
around white folks,
Even with being so-called "woke,"
I tone it down.
Never say "nigga," even when it tries to force
itself out of my lips due to comfortability.
Never sing my favorite rap song too hard.
Never try to be aggressive.
Never try to be angry.
Like I don't have shit to be angry about.
Like I don't have a reason to scream
Or be scared
Or to hate them.
Do I hate them?
I don't know.
My momma ain't raise me like that.
She ain't raise me to be cold,
Or to have hatred.
But I do.
I see them and I hate them.
I don't know them.
I see them and I hate myself
For hating them.
For being mad at them for things they can't
control.

"Don't be like that, don't be judgmental."
Yet they'll kill me for something I can't control.
Like I don't have shit to be angry about.
Like I don't have a reason to hate.
Like I don't have a reason to scream.
Like I don't have a reason to cry.
Like I don't have a reason to be scared,
For my brothers,
For my sisters,
For myself.
So I'm angry,
And I hate,
I hate them.
I hate myself for hating them.
I hate them even more for making me hate them.
My momma ain't raise me like that,
To be cold, to have hatred.
I was raised to be nice.
I am nice .
But I don't wanna be.
I hate them.
I hate them for thinking I should be nice.
I hate them for making me feel like I should be nice.
Nice? Nice?
Nice will get you killed.
Nice will get you laughed at.
Nice ain't doing shit for the black community.
Nice ain't putting these killers in jail.

Nice ain't taking away from them like they have
taken from us,
Making them feel the pain that we feel.
Pain black mothers feel, having their babies
killed on camera for them to never unsee.
Nice?
I can't be nice.
I imagine the thoughts/plans that Ahmaud
Arbery had to come home after his run,
The plans of Sandra Bland, Eric Garner,
Atatiana Jefferson, Rekia Boyd, Alton Sterling
& I think,
When will the day come that I plan to come
home & never make it back?

For Juice

Juice,
I look back on your body of work
Your life and your thoughts.
Girl, you have been through so much.
I don't say that because I'm looking at a victim.
I'm not even speaking about you being a survivor.
I'm talking about the vulnerability and honesty you've shared.
Through the trauma, you've found a way to share your pain with your head held high.
It's admirable.
But one thing I would like you to try is to look past that.
This is not who you are.
Other people's mistakes are not your only story.
Their burdens are not your cross.
You are light.
You are loud laughs and choked giggles.

You are fresh air after a cramped day in
You are funny, intelligent, and powerful
You are not suicide letters, crying nights, and overthinking thoughts.
You don't need to be anyone else.
Your words don't need to sound like anyone else.
Your voice is someone's lullaby.
Your laugh is the soundtrack to someone's life.
Your moan is someone's favorite taste.
Your mind is someone's idea of home.
You are the world, baby girl.
You are the main character, the co-star, and the extras.
You deserve every true thing your heart desires.
Happiness is out there, waiting for you to touch it,
For you to taste its honeyed goodness from its core.
You can have it if you choose.
And it is a choice for only you to choose!
You decide.
But allow yourself to feel it,
To enjoy it.
Everyone else has enjoyed a piece of your beautiful soul.
It's time for you to enjoy it too.

With love,
Jasmine

An updated ode to black women

Sistas,
Thank you for creating and upholding a culture that keeps this world alive.
Thank you for never being one thing, but being everything.
Thank you for dark skin, light skin, white skin, olive skin, and so on,

Because we know you make all.
Thank you for your weaknesses as well as your strengths,
Because your failures may help someone else win.
Thank you for mothering your community, with or without children of your own.
Thank you for being a fresh scalp before school and a greased face in the morning.
Thank you for the late nights and overworked bones.
Thank you for those years in school to become that first.
Thank you for being one of the most educated groups in the country.
Thank you for being trendsetters.
Thank you for being school educated women, entrepreneurs, 304's, sex-working women, religious women, GED women, career driven women, stay-at-home women, fast-food-working women, hard women, soft women.
Because you are all amazing.
You are all beautiful.
You are all seen.
You are all needed.
And if one thing is for certain,
With two things for sure,
They could never do any of this
Without any of you.

Top Shelf

"I'm not coming off the top shelf, just because
you can't reach it."
- Unknown

It took me a while to see myself for the gift that
I am,
And I say that with all humbleness.
Took me a little minute to realize that not
everyone can afford to have expensive taste.
That not every luxury should be available to
every person,
Especially when they have done nothing to
deserve it.
You gotta protect your energy, babygirl.
You gotta guard what's most precious.
And letting one of these trifling-ass niggas steal
your shine,
Damage your aura,
And fuck up your pH balance, just ain't it.
Letting someone rob you of your joy because
they can't create their own sunshine, just
ain't it.
Letting someone lie, cheat, and hurt you, just
ain't it.

Letting someone do the bare minimum for your
love, just ain't it.
Letting someone shame you for being a force
they cannot handle, just ain't it.
Stay on that shelf, mamas.
Because a real one gonna climb up,
and instead of bringing you down, they gone
stand up there with you.

It’s not personal

Don’t take it personal.
Let people be who they are.
It’s not on you to fix.

My choice

Now, this might sound like something stupid.
Might be something you've already realized.
But for me, even at 30, it's not only just clicking,
but I'm just now actually putting it into motion.

But I realize now, that I have choices.
And that I can say no.
Without guilt.
Without explanation.
I can move on from a situation that no longer
serves me.

And that's okay
I can use my PTO days at work without allowing my boss to guilt me into coming in.
I can say no to coming to family events where my abuser will be loved out loud and my trauma will be hushed.
I can speak about my story without telling myself that it's all in my head.
I can choose to be a victim.
Or to not be.
I can choose to be seen.
To be heard.
Or to be felt when I wanna feel.
I can say no to tasks that I am not rightfully paid for.
I can ask for more.
I can.
I have choices.
And it's the most beautiful realization I've ever had.

Wtf (Work To Feel)

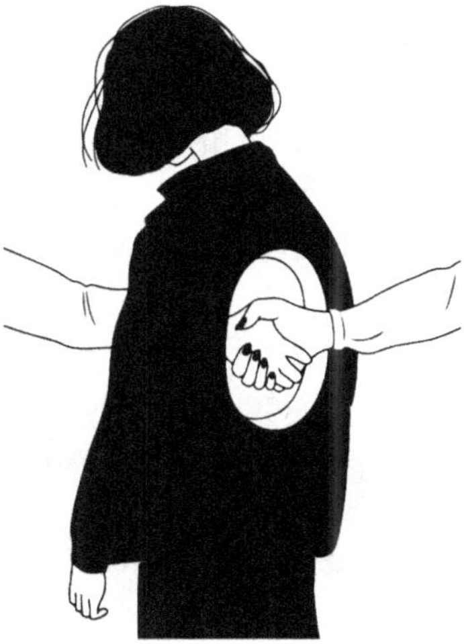

So, I found out that my ex-boyfriend, who was
staying with me and my momma, that I
also was still fucking, but didn't want, was
creeping with another woman.
From a job he didn't even have for a month—
A job that took him our entire relationship to
get.
A job I cried over at night because he wouldn't
apply, wouldn't go to an interview,
Even after watching me give my last to rent,
groceries to feed our bellies,
Or whatever other expense I paid for us.

When I asked him why?

How?
He could betray me in a way after all I'd given,
His answer was simple:
That he wanted to feel good.
He wanted a space to be his happy self because around me, he could not.
I was too much of a reminder of how less of a man he was.
How he was constantly failing.
I wondered if he thought I felt good?
If it felt good to be both man and woman in our relationship?
To cut out all my guilty pleasures and meaningful enjoyment so that we could afford
What we needed?
To lose myself in us because he could only do him?
To become someone I'd never recognized before?
To give,
To give,
To give,
And to never receive?
This man worked a job for one month and instead of creating a thousand ways to make me happy,
He finds another woman and gives it to her,
As if giving me what I deserve is a gift he still cannot afford.

Where's the milk?

Alilah Sheffield once tweeted, "I'm starting to
feel like God went out to get milk…"
And I wondered if God was stopped by the
police on His way,
Maybe got questioned for wearing the wrong
thing,
For walking on the wrong side of the street.
Maybe he stopped for one stranger in need and
ended up getting a line of people who
required more than a loaf of bread and two fish.
Maybe we're just under the impression that God
owes us way more than he's already
Given us.
Maybe we're the ones who went out to get the
milk,
And God is just waiting for us to find our way
back home.

2024 Election

If I stood behind a podium and called you nasty
names, would you vote for me?
If I mocked your child's disability, would you
vote for me?
If I grabbed you by your pussy, would you vote
for me?
If I said the 5 innocent boys in your
neighborhood needed to be murdered, would
you vote for me?
If I sexually assaulted your sister, would you
vote for me?

If I sent your elderly parents back to where they
came from because they're ruining this
great American country, would you vote for me?
If I didn't support women having the right to
their bodies, you having your own right to
your body, would you vote for me?
If I was a woman, if I was black, if I was
anything other than a white bigoted racist
promising to erase anything from this country
that's not what I believe in, would you vote
for me?
You wouldn't.
You just wouldn't.

You're worthy my nigga

Just because you've gotten your hands a lil dirty
And your feet are calloused as fuck
Doesn't mean the journey ain't worthy of being praised
Your time is coming
Your end is near
And when it gets here you may be dirtier than some black Air Force Ones that need to be retired
But you're still worthy, my nigga
And you better not forget it.

www.ingramcontent.com/pod-product-compliance
Lightning Source LLC
Chambersburg PA
CBHW051735130826
49812CB00033B/864
* 9 7 8 9 3 6 3 3 0 1 3 3 7 *